# ESSENTIAL EXISTENTIALISM

~

## the meaning of life

### an Anthology

*Creative Talents Unleashed*

Anthologies Published by Creative Talents Unleashed

All Proceeds from our anthologies are donated to the Starving Artist Fund which helps publish authors at no cost. For more info please visit

www.ctupublishinggroup.com/starving-artist-fund.html

# GENERAL INFORMATION

Essential Existentialism

**By**

Creative Talents Unleashed

1st Edition: 2018

This Publishing is protected under Copyright Law as a "Collection". All rights for all submissions are retained by the Individual Author and or Artist. No part of this publishing may be Reproduced, Transferred in any manner without the prior **WRITTEN CONSENT** of the "Material Owner" or its Representative Creative Talents Unleashed.

*Creative Talents Unleashed*

www.ctupublishinggroup.com

**Publisher Information**
**1st Edition: Creative Talents Unleashed**
**info@ctupublishinggroup.com**

ISBN-13: 978-1-945791-59-8 (Creative Talents Unleashed)

# CREDITS

### Book Cover

Raja Williams

### Creative Director

Brenda-Lee Ranta

### Editor

All Writer's Responsible For Own Work

### Foreword

Brenda-Lee Ranta

# Foreword

**Why are we here?**
**What is our purpose?**
**What is the meaning of life?**

These are the questions that have plagued humanity since the dawn of time.

With the recent passing of *Stephen Hawking*, one of the most world-renowned physicists, known for his enormous contributions to quantum mechanics and general relativity, one has to only look to his astounding life of physical challenges and dedication to finding the answers to these questions. It begs us to continue to look for our own answers.

Within each of us lives the profound potentiality for greatness, capacity to change our world, while finding our own true meaning and purpose on our brief sojourn through time. It is also a personal subject matter, as we are all within ourselves, asking what we are all about as individual persons.

This anthology is dedicated to what gives life meaning and purpose personally. On a grander scale, what is the purpose of our existence as humanity? It is both deeply personal and widely introspective; yet it is also subjective.

Various poets share their verse, prose and poetry about what they perceive to be ***the meaning of life.***

*Brenda-Lee Ranta*

*Apply yourself both now and in the next life. Without effort, you cannot be prosperous.*

*Though the land be good, you cannot have an abundant crop without cultivation.*

*Plato*

# Table of Contents

*Look up at the stars and not down at your feet. Try to make sense of what you see, and wonder about what makes the universe exist.*

*Be curious.*

*Stephen Hawking*

# The Message of Breath

That first breath announced,
with a cacophony of wailing.
In youth,
a pretty girl passes by,
takes his breath away,
albeit for short time.
Suffering twilight years,
out of breath with growing frequency,
distances walked lengthen with age.
The top of the staircase
might as well be Mount Olympus.
Then the last breath,
the death rattle always so unexpected,
in spite of its inevitability.
Breathing defines us as living.
Exercise, sensuality, anxiety quickens breath.
Sleep or spiritual harmony deepens it.
This is our message,
sent out into the world.
We are here, we are here.


*Linda Imbler*

# Nocturnal Sun

There, where the wind fades away
The sky waves its own branches
Retouching icy mornings
In the shades,
Blackbirds and pigeons flapping
And disturbing the sky.
I aimlessly wander through.

Every corner evokes
Spiral lines of perpetually
Ever written sonnets,
Unveiled brides
Blur the color lines
Upon vacant altars.
I become chrysalis
Under the chaos of progress.
I extend my hands
And find only emptiness.
Where do these streets lead me to?
I try to jump over my shadow,
Gradually move
From green to yellow…
Exorbitant looks
Lacking everything
And nothing at all.
In the swinging mist
Every step reflected upon
Its own reflection,
When the twilight expands
I force myself to take shortcuts
That lead me nowhere.

Broken hearts,

Moon's usurped glow,
Yielding ghosts
To the impregnable shine
Of window cars.
Stillness moves,
Static seconds,
Silence declines,
I emigrate with no belongings;
Brittle and gloomy spectrum
De-kernelling good-byes.

My mind is on hold,
Stars cry about
Humidity's shortage
And eclectic rains,
My voice drowns.
Blink away
The ethereal fire of my eyes,
I release myself from prejudice.
I release myself
From body and soul
As nocturnal sun
Amidst the desert.


*Alicia Minjarez Ramírez*

# The Meaning of Life

Experience, explore, embrace
All that becomes
All that is taken away
A brief moment in time
A long pause as you catch your breath

A seed, a sapling, a bud, a tree
Life grows in stages
Big bursts, small movements - time passes
Never knowing where it will take us

A moment passes in the blink of an eye
Did you see it?
Capture it in your life's photo album?

Did you feel the emotions?
Let them fill you up with life's momentum?

Life is memories, opportunities, growth, and love


*Amanda J. Evans*

# Pareidolia

On the moon's craggy canvas,
our brains brushstroke a face
with droopy lids and fleshy smile
from craters and ancient lava flows.

We spot Demeter on a russet,
the Virgin Mary in a quesadilla,
Our Lady of Lourdes on an oak bark,
reclining woman as Mt. Tamalpais,
amazons battling cumulus nimbus,
a smiley face emoji on Venus.

We cannot help but to make things up,
turn Rorschach projections
into angels and clowns—
even the fin of a fish left on a plate
is devoured by a Michelin star
in the squint of an eye,

as we interpret and redefine
the world through imagination,
finding meaning where we make it,
making meaning where we find it.


*Andrena Zawinski*

# Death is Certain

Daily stressing on the cost of living.
They keep raising the prices with no second thought given
I'm still unemployed.
Plagued by these intimate intricate thoughts,
These simple complex dots on the scatter plot.
What is good and what is evil?
What is money worth and
What is success?
What is justice and what is righteousness?
What is love?
Land of the free,
Mind me,
I'm still colonized.
Minority strategized and had the vast majority
marginalized,
And food for thought can't fill the bellies of African babies.
Lost generation
I'm starring at the ceiling, seeing the Earth
Formless and void and no spirit hovering.
Thinking:
Would be Biko be proud of me?
Would Hani come back one more time just to fight for me?
Imagine if Martin never had a dream or
If Malcom had never been to prison.
Driven into a deeper mind-set 'till I'm rudely interrupted.
I'm being told that it's time for church
But I don't want to hear the preacher preach.
Demons stealthily dragging me out, back to hell.
The church be chanting hymns.
I'm more concerned with why the black birds sing.
I learned the song with my headphones on –
Cruising through galaxies,
Escaping reality's

Woes.
Came face to face with the truth and the honesty,
The question being:
Why are we so persistent in doing this "living" thing?
Always on our toes
Could it be the fear of what's not seen?
That death is certain and on our heels?


*Tri*

# Let the Music Play

What is life but a chaotic loop of music,
Without any synchronized beat or rhythm.
Don't search for any meaning, beginning or end,
You will lose your track in this loud noise.
Just follow others on the dance floor.
Look at them!
How they are making futile attempts of dancing.
Shaking their limbs like a zombie.
There are human bones scattered on the floor,
Of those who danced earlier and no more.
Nobody cares, the dance goes on,
As if under a deep spell,
A long cry can be heard from generations to generation.
Let the music play.


*Animesh Das*

# Disconnected

delusions are meaningful explanations for those
who are searching for the significance of life -
a jumble of disconnect faces
slipping in succession
through cracks in the wall
of distant future
ruptured minds are drowned
and wasted in black nights
they wander in clouds of unhappiness -
ponder about the aberration of love
and take walks
on the wild side
bare breasted storms become overdue
as emotions have been kept prisoner
far too long by mental cruelty -
abandoned in cold cells that smell of piss
and bitter sweat that float through
nightmares of madness
in complex minds
life is going at a fast pace
- in reality, without them in it -
lost jewels in a jungle of weeds they are
caught in cobwebs
of misconception

*Jeanette Nel le Roux*

# A Thought is an Idea in Transit

The world is living memory without thought
Music has an unlimited number of percussions
For us, there are all manner of repercussions
Precursors that like birdsong changes, and

Resonates into all spheres all individualities
Therein it attracts expands and contracts
So, it is we ask of our infant minds, why
Why does Pythagoras not answer us?

Why didn't abacus calculate this for us?
Dark matter, energy, matter our solid matter.
Why does it, only amount to a measly 4%?
I guess that's why the god particle, was sent.

It obliterates and yet it now immeasurably
Creates expands its music across the universe
Its true gravity is thought to be infinite
It is a singularity that began as a single note.

It sang the first OM, OM, OM…
If music be the food of love, play on.


*Mark Andrew Heathcote*

# A Prayer for the Prey

The sky is a mouth wide open,
waiting for whoever wanders down the lane
(you'll do in a pinch).

That's what became of Ruth,
tidy, quiet, cheerful little Ruth.
Even though a bag of seven wood lice was buried
to appease the famished arms of the old ash tree.

You see, you've only got one chance –
in fact, five seconds to make a first impression.
So, look closely into the venomous eyes.
Will your interests or wishes prevail over theirs?
Or will you be too easy,
too easy to tear, crunch, chew and swallow?

Hear the creeping in the bushes
followed by grrs, snarls and/or roars?
See the nostrils flare and mouth salivate
as lights flee into strange filaments
with no relation to the dark?

Because mother protects her baby, she's eaten by the fox.
When baby gets to water, he's swooped up
and gulped down by a seagull.
Meanwhile, the 180 million rats bred annually
for America's pet reptiles
do not satisfy demand.

Nevertheless, prepare for your party.
Use sudsing action
to make synthetic cotton clean.
Throw expired cans of soup into the mix.

Chop, season, shake and bake
(as if desirable characteristics
will be -- no, *must* be -- legitimately rewarded).

But no one shows up
because of something you are or are not.
Or because your prey responded
before your stimulus, thus avoiding
the consequence of the stimulus.
After all, someone has to look bad
to make others appear less bad.
Someone has to be fettered in the field
to protect the crops from thunder and hail.

Your mother did the best she could.
God did the best He could.
You also, perhaps, did your best.

So, there's nothing to be afraid of.
Pretend you're surrounded
not by teeth, claws, intestines and shit --
but by golden light.
Tell yourself that you're important --
that you've got a customer and satisfy a need
even if the need is to taste like fresh, buttered corn.


*Paul Brucker*

# Trembling Toward the Sun

How much distance and difference is there
between a mountain and a molehill?

And how far are you determined to climb
to insure your problems amount to blessings in the end?

How tenacious is your will to peace?
How deep is your reservoir of faith?

When you weep with me
do so not out of sorrow
but exultation
and know that even in our suffering
there shines a light of salvation.

How many skeletons are there living in your closet
that rattle bones when you can't sleep at night?

And how tired are the dragons that guard the secrets
hiding in the shadows that haunt your soul?

How dedicated is your tongue to truth?
How strong is your resolve in the fire?

When you dance with me
do so not in half steps
but full measure
and know that every movement
guides us closer to the stars.

How many millstones hang around your neck
as you drag your cross from earth to sea to sky?

And how many psalms do you recite in darkness
as a prayer for healing to arrive with dawn?

How inspired is your passion?
How embedded is your urge to ascend?

When you sing with me
do so not in low key
but high spirits
and know that this language of lyrics
is born of revival.

*Scott Thomas Outlar*

# Into the Beyond

Feels like I'm sinking,
in the cold quicksand,
of age and doubt
The Ides of confusion,
passed unnoticed,
leaving footprints,
in the warm sand,
of someone's memory

Feels like I'm floating,
down northern streams
The scent of new babies,
old stories, happy endings
Drifting ever faster,
approaching the land,
of waterfall rainbows
Cascading into the beyond

Feels like I'm falling,
through familiar voices
Stars casting shadows,
over sunny skies
Questions are asking,
answers are fleeting
Everyone keeps falling,
into the beyond

*Hugh Dysart*

# Mindfulness

So often, life tries to drag us down,
bad decisions, death, illness, love…
Tranquillity, seems out of reach,
dangling from a string up above.
Circumstances change, in seconds,
Joy to gloom, in the blink of an eye.
Balance is found in those moments
when we give peace, another try.
Being mindful of our situation,
brings us back to our own truth.
So often, we shift blame to others,
because it is the easiest thing to do.
Awareness of our own actions,
takes unhappiness back to source.
We can change today's outcome,
by restoring our thought's course.
Towards the path of enlightenment,
fear diminishes, blame weakens.
Joy overcomes doubt, love prevails,
in those moments, life truly begins.
Serenity is mine, it is yours as well,
the doors of the past are closed.
My intentions are guided by love,
on a path, my soul already knows.

*Debra McLain*

# Office Plant

Martine walked along the street looking up at the
streetlights. The full moon stared down at her bent head.
"Why look up?" She thought, following her feet with her
eyes.

"The world is round, God is good. So what!"
She continued to walk remembering her job and the endless
desks under endless windows looking over endless
sidewalks going to endless skies in the distance.

"So what! Why believe in anything?" She said out loud to a
watching tree. Looking up at the moon, she gave it the
finger. "Life just is. I dare you to change my mind."
The moon seemed to wink.

"Huh?" She shook her head to try to clear it.
"I've read Sartre, Kierkegaard and Campus.
I read Nietzsche even though he was a Nazi sympathizer.
I know what's absurd. Me, for wanting something more."
She told herself, stamping her foot.

"I won't tell anyone that I'm just another office plant, nearly
dead, looking out a sunny window, hoping for something."

Martine sighed and walked on.


*Glenda Higgins*

# The Hallucination of Nonexistence

Access to the axis of excess of thought.
You expressed disappointment at this
particular point in the appointment.
I noticed a hesitant resentment immanently
resonant like an aura's transcendent
remnant emanates over the interstate
into the Pool of Placation and beyond
into the Ethnosphere's massive congregation
of Mankind's situation
of the Suchness of this transmission's importance
as far as interpretation of the possibility
of a simultaneous deathful lifelessness.


*Heath Brougher*

# Acts of the Will

As you steer towards becoming of
age, you need to set up your own stage
all the guidance in your heavy
case, cannot determine your final settling down place
You pick up chunks of advice along the
way, still you need to work your own clay
shaping it day after
day, not allowing others viewpoints to get in the way
You are the leader of your own
pack, while your will refuses other parties influence attack
your backbone holds up your
back, therefore you don't allow anyone to crack
Through your willpower so
strong, as both of you stroll along
busy determining right from
wrong, figuring out where you belong
The act of your will must take
responsibility, and shape the person you'll be in society
this is our biggest
reality, irrespective the ties to your family

*Bevan Boggenpoel*

# Meaning of Life

The existence of an individual life
Means nothing without variables,
Choices,
Chances,
Mutations.
The meaning of death
Essentially the same thing,
But the meaning of life
Is everything in between.
The smile-the frown.
The darkness-the light.
The hardness-the kindness.
The love-the hate.
It's not what you obtain,
But what you give of yourself
And leave behind.


*Debra Sasak Ross*

# An Examination of Thy Mind

The human mind, an innate, yet intricate tool
with bountiful unique thoughts and often persistent inquiry
that lead us to unanswered conundrums to untangle.

There are whispers of intense phrases,
which leave us petrified, a real fear to say such aloud.
We panic, with anxiety, trying to unravel those hidden
secrets
that are buried beneath our young wise souls,
with answers that tremble upon our quivering lips.

Inside, our heart ticks, trying to express outward,
as we hunker down inward…
Words forcing their way through a dry mouth…

"Dear soul, what is this life?
Why do we live such and then die?"

"My love, if I am to betroth you till the day I die,
then why, why, do we fall asleep, and I leave you so lonely,
into the midnight nigh?"

"I fear, that one day, all of this radiant magical beauty of
nature,
I shall be robbed of,
But my love, I have undying faith, that there is thy God,
who shall be waiting for thee….
and he will journey me into divine green pastures…"

Oh, so I sing,
my heart turns and turns,
even if the questions I ask my heart, they do sting

but I seek truth in which I search for mercy.

This life, such an intricate life, vast universe
My heart desires for a place that thee will call home,
a castle in the sky
somewhere where dark is no longer nigh.

I do request, just this,
as I wear my open heart upon my chest,
do not leave me lonely, for I have betrothed to thee

My heart, shall forever beat,
in all eternity.


*Ariana R. Cherry*

# Daily Bread

Maybe that's my lesson for today,
to hold on to the simple moments.
Appreciate them a little more as
there's not many of them left now.
I don't ever want that for you.
Finding things that make you happy
shouldn't be so damn hard.
I know you'll face pain and suffering.
Hard choices will rear their heads.
You can't let the weight of the bad
choke the joy out of your life.
No matter what, you have to find those
things that love YOU and run to them.
There's an old saying, "that which doesn't
kill you will make you stronger."
I don't believe that, I think the things that
try to kill you make you angry and sad
turning you into a cynic and non-believer.
Strength comes from the good things,
your family, your friends. Your faith and
satisfaction in work and play.
Those are the things that will keep you
whole, those are the things to hold onto
when you feel broken. Those are the
things that will keep you centered.


*Ken Allan Dronsfield*

# Fire at Will

We live a life
"Feuer Frei"
With words that hurt
Cause for us to cry
The trust we share
In laws and belief
Has given us burning grief
For the life we live
Comes with a price
Freedom and free will
Are silent lies

We live a life
"Feuer Frei"
A Nation's idealist massacre
The life of freedom in this nation
Has been born of segregation
The only way to survive this life
Is to live it "Feuer Frei"

Keep the weak on their knees
The institutional gain
For the blood that runs
In each one's veins
Isn't always seen the same
The life we live shows a lie
Seen with blinded eyes
As freedom and dreamers
Paint the sky
A life to live
"Feuer Frei"

*Markus Fleischmann*

# Some Days Love

Some days
I am overwhelmed
how precious
our love
by what grace
whose divine power
was it this blessed Mother Earth
or the universe itself
who am I to thank
for giving little old me
this opportunity
this adventure
this awakening
that life can get better
than your best imaginings
how do I repay
do I honor
this gift
now I understand
I must value myself
I must believe I am worthy
live my life convinced I deserve this breath
that's all that's asked in return.


*Roz Weaver*

# Divination

I lay my meager offerings
at the altar of the universe
My piteous actions
can never compare
to the wonders of
that from which I
was born, mysteries
await my rediscovery
for these parts of myself
lay asleep and unknown
yet, still I remain tethered
to your wonders, my heart
whispering this truth

My mortal life be my
humble offering, till
my return to what is
the endless awareness
and celestial splendor,
birthed in divination
and love,
yes!
Blessed love.


*Brenda-Lee Ranta*

# Life

Life.
What is it worth
Is it a gift to some
And a bane to others.

It seems to be taken so lightly
Thrown away at the slightest notion
While some try to improve their lot in it
Others take it without a thought

A baby is born
A new life begins
But will they live to enjoy it
Or will another one leave
Before their time

An elder coming to the end
A life lived long
Yet his life feels incomplete
No more will he teach the young

We take our own lives
For reasons sometimes unknown
Why would you kill someone
Just because you want a pair of shoes

We lose our lives
To the ones sworn to protect
In compliance even though we maybe
It doesn't seem like to anyone
Our lives seem to matter.

*Anthony Arnold*

# Insights

Taciturn I roam
In the sterile fury
Of delirium,
Carry my words
As single luggage.

Behind me…
Drive my inconclusive
Dreams, pain,
Blind nostalgia.
Diluting rain
Concentrating
My footsteps.

The wind recounts
It´s story.
I wait for
The glaring spikes
On diaphanous voices,
Coated with infinity.


*Alicia Minjarez Ramírez*

# Our Meaning of Life

Our energy
our essence
our will
we go on strong
our fire
our desire
the place that we belong
our growth
our heart
the lifeblood through our veins
our entities fly high
our excitement through the rain.

Our meaning of life
our ambitions and spirt
a constant cycle of survival
that comes with sacrifice
our meaning of life
through our trials and tribulations
there's happiness through suffering
there's knowledge and participation
in our meaning of life.

Our human condition
our personalities
the hands we've been dealt
our biography
our history
the stories that we tell
our confessions
our lies
our ability to adapt
and change with the times.

Our meaning of life
our ambitions and spirt
a constant cycle of survival
that comes with sacrifice
our meaning of life
through our trials and tribulations
there's happiness through suffering
there's knowledge and participation
in our meaning of life.

The lifeblood through our veins
our entities fly high
there's excitement through the rain.

Our meaning of life.


*Jeff Oliver*

# Evolution in Resolution

Evolution of the body
Revolution of the mind
Look for heaven above the stars
Seek and ye shall find
There is more that we don't know
Then we've already established
So maybe God can be explained
In terms of quantum physics
Focus on a single star
Consider the source of this light
And realize the beautiful mysteries
That shines in the sky at night


*Kimmy Alan*


*Inspired by Hoag's Object; taken by Hubble Telescope*

# Where is My Place

I creased the page
to mark my place,
but when I returned
the fold had disappeared
and I was unsure,
unsure
if I had found it.
I scratched my head and pondered,
was it really my place?
the place
I'd once inhabited in times past.
It didn't seem quite right.
Perhaps I'd moved on too quickly,
turned over two pages instead of one.
Perhaps I should go back,
retrace my steps
rethink
where I should be.
Rethink
where I should look.
Rethink
where I should look to find
my place.


*Lynn White*

# The Machine

The Machine rose from the ashes of my exploded mind
spraying paint of creativity across the globe.
One by one those that were created before
became infected by floating essence of pure vision.

With the speed of a ravenous cheetah
fertile imagination rolled across stale pastures
like an avalanche of snow down the tallest mountain
leaving none immune to its glorious awakening.

But the machine that spawned was dark,
darker than the deepest pit of the abyss.
And it went forth across those pastures
sowing seeds of vexation into the ground.

Thus, was born the instrument of self-doubt
dispersed amongst life's cattle
as cherry blossom in a windswept garden
on a scorched spring morning.

Alas aspiration lingered in the pollinated breeze
fusing to every consciousness it encountered,
creating the everlasting sanctuary of dreams
where fruitful imaginings transcend prosaic thought.

*Matthew John Lambert*

# Reflections and Shadows

Sitting here by the pool,
the light shifting the shadows,
watching the reflections of the trees and plants,
on the surface of the pool
I go deep within my soul
and breathe in the cool air,
filling my lungs with the breath of life
Knowing that I'm like the tress and the plants,
ever changing
in the light and the shadows
Gratitude wells up in my heart
For there are so many things to be grateful for
To the Universe and its Creator
I give thanks and praise


*Jill N. Pontiere*

# Searching

If we are searching,
then we are lost.
If we are lost,
what are we searching for?
Is it an old man with a beard?
Is it our father or mother?
Are we searching for the womb,
the cocoon, before freedom's flight
lost our way?
Maybe we aren't lost.
Maybe we haven't been found,
as our reflection
is where we're bound
and the mirror is all around;
it's in the crown,
controlling the ground.
It's in a sound.
It's in a scent,
whose taste can't hide
from who generates inside,
and we can't go back
for future pride.
We're already on the ride
so, ease the dis-ease.
The only cost to pay
in a pocketful of miracles,
is our attention,
where the past, present,
and future all meet;
for there's nowhere
to be but, now here.

*Justin R. Hart*

# Music of the Medusa

One being, a bell with tentacles, having already designed and imagined all that exists, except for the best of musical sounds, sent every tentacle to travel through space, to travel through time, requesting each realm to develop their own unique sound, asking each world to discover that single note and keep it safe until the tentacle could return and learn it and return to the Medusa with that sound on its tongue.

A tone to be added to a magnificent composition so that all places might share in a great song, enjoy divine, melodic bliss. So, having been informed of the task, the music of the spheres began. Each world constructed Schelling's frozen music and taught the sound to their children so that they could connect with nature and all that she provides.

On our own world, man sang, but he found legion and each became unknown to the others, a free will gift. So, in time, there was much dissonance, too many sounds, all so different, and out of harmony. Discord became the status quo. But one day, Earth's tentacle will return and ask as it was instructed, for our world to provide, as one tongue, a single intonation that is striking, melodious, benevolent.

For our sake, Mankind will have to find that voice together. For at the last and at the beginning, the Medusa, that source of all beauty that any have ever known or dreamt of, will combine all sounds, even it, which man, as one world, composed, and will create a symphony of the ages, which will never cease.

*Linda Imbler*

# Infinity Attired

It's the nectar of your body that I love, & nightly smell,
the film of saline gloss, where your belly starts to swell,
It's the drop of beaded dew, upon your downy upper lip,
those runnels upon your skin, that drip below your hip.

It's the oasis where your armpit, embraces rounded breast,
ripples of sweet elixir, that lets no man sleep, nor ever rest,
that mustiness of living, slaking tired soul & errant tongue,
whence from bed sheet & body, every droplet's duly rung.

It's the moisture of our loving, cracking drought's hard
shell, rivulets slow-snaking, into inner thigh's soft &
deepest well, the sweat upon your brow, & behind your
bent rounded knee, the perspiration from your pores, is my
slicked & salted sea.


*Sue Lobo*

# Destiny Intertwined

For the reason that
we numb our aching hearts
shield our deepest thoughts
paint over the mirror of our spirit
then close our self into a cocoon of indifference.
We limit our prospective
to a nearsighted view of our surroundings
a close-minded intolerance to change
in preference for shifting the blame.
We surrender to live within
repeating cycles of irritation,
a never-changing
cascade of circumstance.
We emit incessant vibrations,
which grow to be waves,
that crash upon the distant shores
of other restless souls.
We can choose to be receptive
like we were as a child.
Allowing every breath,
to change our journey in life.
No matter how lost
or alone we feel
we are each indelibly
connected to everyone.
The things we do
immediately change
their future too
in some way.
Our destiny
is intertwined with
the faceless throngs
we ignore.

If we do the same things
as the days that came before
all of our tomorrows will intermingle
with our unfulfilled yesterdays
in an endless procession.


*Valormore De Plume*

# In Just Reaching Out

Find interest in each new day
or you're not living

Release the inner spirit
once you have found it

Lend another a hand
restore simple things

Others won't trip
if you show them the way

For just the one reaching out
starts to make the world new


*Ken Green*

# Unpredictable

life is a story that tells itself
in silver portals and black wagons
where blue drop spiders reign
and corpses are hidden
in the waste of the night
where black angels
are creatures with
dangerous hearts
and chilling secrets
men live and die - bruised by life
they never quench their thirst
to fulfil their dreams or satisfy
their appetites or desires –
still, rivers will flow
and tides will run
hearts will be drowned
in unpredictable streams
of dwindling happiness

*Jeanette Nel le Roux*

# Existentialism

Connectivity of Earth's productivity
Malign and insane
We are the dark matter that plagues
Festers and grows
In our self-destruction it shows
Life is unity in its purity
Like a web of strands, a chain-link fence
We are the poisonous flow
In the universal vein
We are the cause of our own pain
Like Cancer we attack each other
Eating away at the fundamentals
The reasons of our being
We are the children
Ignorant and unforgiving

We imprisoned ourselves
With religion and faith
Shackled by idealism
Bonded by supremacy
Of our minds free will
We preach and teach
As into the Earth we reach
We plunder, ravage and rape
Our home
On which we are born
Yet called it our own
Life is alive
An unrelenting wrath
We its beings,
Took our last breath

*Markus Fleischmann*

# Blood Red and Lit up like a Rose

Alkalize the sorest spot
where scabs have been ripped away
on purpose
to reveal ancient scars
that tear tissues from the box.

Digging through the shadow spaces
of my own psyche
that long were silenced
because this time I brought
ten thousand lights
to shine at the ceremony.

The older I get
the easier it becomes to forget
pains of the past
but I don't want to
because every time I churn the soil
where regrets lie dormant
I want to renew a prayer
of forgiveness
that creates a brighter path
blazing into the future.

Cut the music!
Place a dozen red roses
with thorns removed
atop every grave.
This is a day
to hear the birds sing
after the rain.

Walking along the soggy earth

where footing remains solid
because even if the sun
is resting behind gray clouds
my vision remains as clear
as his smile before the final breath.

Drain the system of toxic plumes
that fog the mind
with poison
and scorch the blood
with living fire
from the truth
that offers salvation.

Cue the music!
This is a day
to dance through fields
where seeds are soon to sprout.
This is the hour
to bask in lessons
that teach of faith without doubt.


*Scott Thomas Outlar*

# Revelatory, Version II

In this world of heartless consumption
waste of human life to the whipsaw;
children shot dead while at recess
never did so little mean so much
then when two deer in a field
saw you and you saw them
nothing else mattered...
as neither blinked.
Self-righteous take aim.
the pious obey at the sight
non-believers glare but afraid
Little flakes of shimmering light,
Admiring all in the wafting shade,
Stars peek and rave in the delight;
stellar was how a twilight was made,
As all eyes peer at the lightened cross.


*Ken Allan Dronsfield*

# The Pilgrim on A Journey

**I.** I am a pilgrim on a mission's journey,
my life is an open book to everyone I meet
the end I still can't see for my tavern,
is hidden in a deserted place
only embedded in my mystic dreams.

**II.** From each road I traversed on,
I met extraordinary people
from an ordinary world we inhabit
a vagabond touched my life with his stories
of life's bitter-sweet scenes, a lonely soul pierced my heart
for the longing to find himself in a whirlwind of maze-like
obscurities on his every path....

**III.** The question is always the same, "where is my place in
this world?" where can I finally find myself for I have been
lost a dozen of lifetimes before, with the cyclical
reincarnation of my perturbed soul
Can you please tell me where is my true home?

**IV.** In your journey through life as you meet different
people along your path, you can either teach them
and touch their lives like no one ever did before
Or you could be the one to learn lessons that will be left
embedded in your heart, But goodbye is inevitable like the
chapters of a book, the time comes when things have to
end…

*Elizabeth Esguerra Castillo*

# The Light

I close my eyes in the dark,
so, I can see
Feeling my way along the seams,
of perception
I close my eyes in the dark,
so, I can see the light

I close my eyes in the dark,
so, I can see the music
Melodies in black velvet,
the poetry of ebony skies
I close my eyes in the dark,
so, I can see the light

Sunshine on the living,
the dead come out at night
Tell me all your secrets,
so, I can see the light
Leave me in the morning,
come to me at night
Sing a mother's melodies,
so, I can see the light

I close my eyes in the dark,
to see her face
Her voice calls me home,
to the other side of night
Where my old dog sleeps,
and I can see the light


*Hugh Dysart*

# You are Unique

Open your mind's eye
listen to what it says
Maybe it wants to show you
something you want to digest
It might just steer you
into places you wouldn't believe
Just make sure you are there
where you need to receive
That person you want to become
sometimes controlled by some
But who is stopping you
to pick up your own choices and run
To a private place
where you'll feel free
To that special situation
where you'll for once agree
Being yourself
not conforming to someone else
Away from influences
coming from family and pals
You are unique
you are one of a kind
Don't allow anyone else
to change your healthy mind

*Bevan Boggenpoel*

# Another Summer's End

It was summer yesterday; now it's autumn.
Echoes of departure keep resounding in the air.
—Baudelaire

We trail the water's edge
in step to a buoy's song
on the natural rhythm
of swells and waves and charm.

The sky tonight, streaked
in a wildfire of color,
takes flight on wings
of western gulls.

Like memories love makes
and promises it keeps,
this is how I wish
to remain here, content

to tuck myself inside the beat
of bird wings along this shoreline
walk, to inhabit each other's lives
like our souls do their bodies.

As guests here, let us continue
to wander beneath a low ceiling
of feathered clouds—
long and endless.

Meditation at the Dunes of Asilomar

In all the things of nature
there is something of the marvellous—Aristotle

Trumpets of desert sand verbena
and leafy coastal sage wort nestle in

with paintbrush and seaside daisies,
ageless blooms at home in the dunes

inside the whip of wind and weight of fog,
facing the rocky cove's icy tides and surf.

Beneath a sky a spray of constellations,
lovers pass by snuggling into each other,

their windswept laughter a night song
drifting past plumes of pampas grass.


*Andrena Zawinski*

# Bittersweet

How weary, a foot can be, placed
One following another
Each one a brother slightly splayed
One following another
But never, truly together!

How, easily can a mind be spliced
Torn roughly apart
Like a peach from its stone—sacrificed.
Ripped roughly apart
But never, with a total, disregard.

How tiresome, a heart can beat
Breath after breath
Not finding a moments breath replete
Breath after breath
Brimming, full but yet full of conceit.

Heavy like golden ears of wheat
We hang our heads
As if life were something obsolete
We hang our heads
Thou others are no less bittersweet.


*Mark Andrew Heathcote*

# Foreshadowing in Life?

Foreshadow-
A warning or indication of a future event.
Throughout our lives, events take place.

We question their timing
the why's
and when
So many questions
lead to impossible conundrums and
we look for clues.

Were we warned?
Did our divine father leave simple hints?
Or were we blind to a truth that we didn't want to see?

Does our life contain foreshadowing?
For our mind to perceive…
Or for perhaps our searching hearts, to feel?

Is our road life mapped out, with foreshadowing planned?
So, we can see the construction up ahead?

Can destiny be twisted?
Or do we ultimately have faith, to let go of the reigns
From time to time?
Will we see the bumps on this trail of life?

There are trials that invade our safe spaces
and revelations that come to dawn…
yet, we move forward,
sometimes too quickly - or not quick enough.

We seek truth

but, will the wisdom escape
from the tip of our silent tongue,
as we await to be carried,
or do we seek the ultimate truth
that is stored in the depths of our heart strings?


*Ariana R. Cherry*

# Purpose of Life

Could death really be just a metaphor for all our fears and
insecurities?
We've personified religion as if it speaks for us.
Divided us into colonies;
Trying to vigorously dictate delicate, intricate philosophies.
So, we delegate priests
To indoctrinate young kids into our idea of:
What's life if it's not…?
What's cool and hot.
What's free and what's bought.
Tell me, what's greed and where does it stop?
This life has taken everything,
My dreams and my sanity.
How am I at fault?
All I've done to daunt you was keeping it real:
We love – we laugh
We hate – we kill and
Still we build
Heal and travel with past pleasant memories.
And probably the most important thing would be that we
LIVE.
If that ain't the purpose, I don't know what is.


*Tri*

# The Game of Life

A game of two halves,
Black versus white
Who will win?
Does it really matter?
Your views, my views
Opinions don't count
Slaves to the adversity – the government rules

Black versus white
Checkmate
We do not see the world
Just the square in front of us
Blind to the corruption
The poison seeping into our minds
Led by the views of others
TV screens, social media, false news

Stretch your thoughts
See through eyes not blinkered
Move two steps not one
Feel your way forward
The heart never lies
Truth is within
Take the time to visit

Black versus white
A game no more
Equal against equal
Game over

*Amanda J. Evans*

# Corporeal and Not Corporeal

Paradox is just Paraguay pirouetting into pixelated post-
mortem—
a perception to be experienced
in the minds of the living,
though does that not constitute existence?
do illusions ripe and real
as reality form an abstraction
of the extant world
no matter how spurious
they are known to be as far as the proportion
of their pathetic plagiarism of life
they may pretend to predominate?


*Heath Brougher*

# Celestial

I see things so beautiful
entrancing and Devine
so heavenly, so humble
an enduring deathless shrine
an arch angelic beauty
not demonic or unkind
I keep my vision radiant
a cerebral euphoric sublime.

We the immortal
we the celestial
hallowed by our time
we the humble
we the innocent
celestial in our minds
an otherworldly transcendent
an infinite glorious Devine.

Though our bodies not everlasting
our hearts will cease to beat
then take us on the journey
of supernatural things
when we leave this earthly prison
immortal and sublime
we now know
we've reached our Devine.

We the immortal
we the celestial
hallowed by our time
we the humble
we the innocent
celestial in our minds

an otherworldly transcendent
an infinite glorious Devine.

Though our bodies not everlasting
our hearts will cease to beat
then take us on the journey
of supernatural things.

Celestial so Devine.


*Jeff Oliver*

# Searching for God

Please tantalize me, with those ancient lost tales,
I ask only that you pleasure me, with poetry scribed,
Tease me with quatrains, & tickle me with trilogies,
And caress me with softly, with cantatas of whales.

Kiss me, with the urgent kindling of ritual's old fires,
Love me longingly & languidly, with lace-clad lyrics,
Adore me, with the chanting of wise hooded Druids,
And play me please, upon strings of harps & old lyres.

Sing me songs of long ago, & those of way back when,
Meld me with melodies, from nightingale's gold nebs,
Pray me within God's prayers, of adoration & homage,
And please make love to me, in ways unknown to all men.


*Sue Lobo*

# Faraway Air

Each sparkle has a distant and severe air.
Dusty breeze undoing
Selfless prejudices,
Diaphanous sky
Of faraway shores.
Untellable words!
Sweet craving that leads
And mitigates nostalgia,
Drunkenness of the moment
Impossible fight
Bold and incandescent soul.
Every sound is a wonderful caress
Momentum, track and halo of a transient light.

Each sparkle has a distant and severe air.
I understand the instant is non-existing matter.
Burns like a wound inscribed within our consciousness,
Affliction goes away.
Full delight of interrogations and absences,
Depths and appearances;
Defining the earthly paradise hell
Of my own communion.

Each sparkle has a distant and severe air.
I learn to live
In the branches of a secret dream,
Of a fiery shade,
In the shortened line
Of abysmal dementia.
Choleric air of ephemeral tears
Shake up my roots.

Lewd whisper
Born from the body,
Proclaiming the cavity
Of long gone solitudes.

*Alicia Minjarez Ramírez*

# Out of the Dust

From deep within the hallowed ground,
souls of men come outward bound.
Formed anew from earthen soil,
lives are spent in constant toil.
Seek we now a higher calling,
than drunkenness and useless brawling.
With open eyes we forward strive,
to make our mark and stay alive.
Aspire to greatness we concoct,
instead, we fill our hearts with rocks.
Unfurling wings, we hope to fly,
to soar with God before we die.
Short, our time, on this rotating stone.
Let's walk upon it, but not alone.
Reach out with love, to those you find,
 remember always, to be kind.
Into earth, we'll go again,
remembered not, in minds of men.
Love we've given, turns not to dust,
God allows it, to stay with us.
The final journey, made alone,
to a place, we'll call our home.
Where everything, is more than nice,
We'll share with Him, true paradise.


*Valormore De Plume*

# Three Words

Three words,
That's all I have
Three words,
To explain it all
How can I put it?
How can I express it?
With truth
Three words
So little, to say so much
Three words
An entire life
Three words
Lived and loved


*Amanda J. Evans*

# Redemption

Crying out for redemption
for sins she can't recall,
the darkest nights lay
cold upon her aching soul

wordless pleas cry out
to bleach her clean by
blinding light, in loves
sweetest deliverance

Bequeathed her wings,
once more by foot,
till flight then ends
her tainted life of plight

*Brenda-Lee Ranta*

# Starry Eyes

The sky is watching
Starry eyes blinking,
thinking of me
Whispering amongst themselves,
feeding my doubts,
starving my faith

The sky is calling
Starry eyes following,
swallowing me whole
Nudging me toward the exits
When this war is over,
everyone goes home

The sky is laughing
Starry eyes twinkling,
sprinkling my ashes
Spreading me across galaxies
Breathing my dust,
sharing my soul

The sky is a symphony
Starry eyes closing,
composing concertos in the dark
Every note a life, every soul a song
Etched into forever's,
rock of ages

The sky is calling


*Hugh Dysart*

# Time and Money

Where does this damn time go?
Is it stored in batteries hidden in
the back of the underwear drawer?
Perhaps stored in a coconut radio
built by the Professor and stashed
by the lagoon on Gilligan's Island.
I think it might disappear into the
land of lost socks.
I feel disheartened as I search
for more.
It tires one out so quickly.
I use more as I search for it.
I try to buy it, but the check always
bounces.
It appears the more of it I have;
the more I seem to spend?
Much like money.... how odd.
All my friends tell me, "you can't
take it with you when you go",
but truthfully, I don't think I'll
have the time to worry!


*Ken Allan Dronsfield*

# Realm of Regrets

There, in the Realm of Regrets, my burdens were heavy, almost intolerable. I observed the faces of everyone I have ever known. Revolving spheres of accusations. Every unkind word, selfish action, or tears I had made another shed, rose up before me. Each orb, a reminder of instances long forgotten, or excused. Overwhelmed and weary, I laid down my pride and collapsed into a heap of regret. My tears floated in the space around me. Each drop, transformed into a bright star, letting me know I had been forgiven for my wrongdoings. An astronomical amount of love overcame me, for others as well as myself. Absolution was mine, and the world around me was more beautiful.

*Debra McLain*

# Veracity

For tiny split of second
Found myself in eternity
And saw facade of mortality

Adage streaming divinity
Within charismatic dynamics
Of morality, right before my eyes

Blissful dynamics of mortality
Jolted my still moment of eternity
Handed me to moment of mortality

From there I glanced back
To my snatched moment of eternity
Found serenity in mesmeric perpetuity

*Muhammad Azram*

# Time Warp

the nothingness is complete -
it gathers like clouds
and shipwrecks time
on islands of doubt
where the past still
lives inside us
tears drum on breasts
(the altars of passion)
but it does not define the darkness inside -
it does not weigh the wild winds
when dust turns
to dust again
even those who still
live in yellowed pictures
of days gone by
have no joy in the now -
endure no burdens
of yesterday
despairing is the concomitant of life
splattered with fragile deceits -
it drifts back and forth
on tides of uncertainties -
anchors are wrenched away
in the time warp of today


*Jeanette Nel le Roux*

# Existence

Am I or am I not, free to be me?
Do I exist or is this only a dream?
I wonder was I ever truly free?
Or am I floundering in the stream?

Does reality explain my existence?
Is there a method to this madness?
Over wroth by constant resistance,
Delusions of happiness or sadness.

If existence does have meaning
I wonder if it can be explained
Will it be a conspiracy convening?
Or is the knowledge simply ingrained.

Our existence is always changing
Unrestrained in the passage of time
Because evolution is rearranging
It has become a never-ending climb.

Your own reality is always different
Depends on your philosophy of life
In whatever direction that you went
To find either happiness or strife.

It starts on the day you were born
The formation your existence begins
With each generation it is reborn
Over time it soon transcends.

*James F. Cunningham*

# Remember

The father of a friend,
Who taught you a lesson.
The meaning of life,
With a lasting impression.
He spoke with a tone,
As a man of his word.
His thoughts in my mind,
Will always be heard.
Give all that you got,
Never giving any slack,
For what you give in life,
Is what you get back....

*Jeffrey D. Keeler*

# Time's Addiction

Initially inebriated
by the labor of birth,
intoxicating Time tracks
our stimulated lives
with tantalizing traces
of exhilarating
euphoric elevations,
arousing a remedy
that shares a substance
for a sensitivity
to vibrate ecstasy
as symptoms of seizures
strike secondary seconds,
and moments malaise
into malady's minutes.
Uncounted hours are ours,
while waiting for days,
though yearning for years
to find faith's fruition
within the duality
of individuality.
Still, our terminal addiction
that tepid Time buys
can only be cured
during death's demise.

*Justin R. Hart*

# We Don't Know

You have your beliefs, & I too, have mine,
Of Heaven & Hell, & also, of what´s Divine,
Our pilgrimages differ, that´s true, I do know,
I do Santiagos Camino, & off to Mecca you go.

You may be ultra this & I, be opposite of that,
We walk diverse paths & we don different hats,
Politics, religion, what´s right, & what´s wrong,
We all sing with same voice, but not to same song.

You think you know best, & also, I think I do too,
But you cannot judge me, & I can never judge you,
We bumble through time, & we age, as winds blow,
And yet the only thing certain, is that none of us know.


*Sue Lobo*

# A Big Time

Fearful that life's but a sad mystery?
Only some find blessed sweet harmony.
Riding on rough tides, it seems, every day?
Even in bad times, have good things to say.
Verify that you are one of a whole,
Even though each plays a small solo role;
Rest your head gently; your soul can't be sold.


*John Lambremont, Sr.*

# Where Are You

Life's journey allows
the destination
to find us
each our own

Do not forget
many paths cross
on different journeys
greet the strangers

Asking as you go
Is this the way
for some choices
are not made by you

Calm the fears
beyond your control
detours are for learning
that destinations change

Allow past steps
knowing they placed you
where you are
supposed to be


*Ken Green*

# The Inner Being

What you grow into
Is determined by you
Religion or community
Don't even have a clue
Though it influences
To a certain amount
What you wish to become
Will always be around
You are nurtured
To a certain age
But as an adult
You write your own new page
The foundations laid
Prepares the way
But the inner being
Is there to stay
It will always intervene
Regularly part of the scene
Grooming your future
It is always keen
Don't even fight
Its massive power
Acknowledge its presence
Like you would a lovely flower
The inner being
Injected into your fiber
Ignoring outside pressure
Lifting your willpower higher

*Bevan Boggenpoel*

# Who are We?

We are the light of moon
Who we are
We are shining stars in darkness
Dreams fail but hope never dies
Who we are
We are humans
From one race
From Eve and Adam
Of different religions but with one God
But no one understands
I believe your conscience still alive
Who we are
We are humans
From one race
We will raise the flag of peace
Together we can have peace
We are shining stars in darkness
Let's raise the flag of peace
For brotherhood and co-existence


*Monsif Beroual*

# Exhaustion Manifest

I'm the manifestation of exhaustion through an iridescent
sphere of discontent
drowning in Gaia's blood freed from cracks in her farm
filling my lungs as I struggle to swim towards the day's
shore.

My shade's light now rests upon a darkened anvil of
destruction
primed for the swift swing of summary execution
by an odious image born from my own restiveness.

Salvation flutters upon air spiraling with unrestricted
abandon
as a leaf on a turbulent autumn afternoon
detached from its now sparse dormant bough.

I breathe deeply inhaling unbounded spiced molecules
infusing my shade with abundant medication of restoration.
Bathed in renewed vigor it returns to my physical self.

Now with defined purpose my vessel may once again
confront the complexity of pilgrimage.


*Matthew John Lambert*

# On-Running Age ~ A Reflection

Sometime I do wonder
About speed and time
Of on-running age
The swiftness of time
And developments
It is amazing but scary
How things and events
Explored in short spin of time
On the stage life and living
How the life is happening
Wondered and amazed
Realities are getting unveiled
Hidden truths are explored
Or earth is heaving them out
From the hidden treasures
Earth and space exploring
All the hidden secrets
Preserved and reserved
From millions of years
And now it is throwing out hastily
Like it sick of hiding them for years
And now throwing all secrets
Or might to expose and explore all
Before expose to no secrets
I do wonder on the haste of truth
What will happen when no secrets left?
On the very dynamic stage of life
As it's happening with rapid speed!


*Muhammad Azram*

# Some Soldier the Storm

Dogwoods bloom white along the side of the street
signaling early scenes of spring to come

Sun shines clear on a bright blue day
No glasses to shield the light
Penetrate my open eyes
Grant me a vision of purpose

A beat-up Ford station wagon
with wood paneling from the 1980's
speeds by as a flash of childhood memories arise

Detox Avenue is no slice of pie in the sky
Red apples spill their juice
to cleanse my blood
and sing their song of life through my liver

Dancing alone on a bridge in the woods
as thoughts of her heart serenade my mind
Each step is a prayer spoken along with a mantra
designed to reduce the distance between

Glistening water gently flows
over rocks made smooth by time
as my soul undergoes a trial by fire

Birds chirp from their perch in the trees
Clue me in on the symphony's secret
Teach me the calm that arrives after storms

Dreams of friends that I haven't seen in years
Dreams of loved ones that could not be saved
rage with an anger I try to understand

Dreams of a past that must be forgiven
Dreams of a future that offers a path forward

Strangers pass by on an afternoon walk
Some smile
Some wave
Some turn away
Some happy
Some healthy
Some broken on their cross
in this world that can be so cruel

Two squirrels chase each other
through the leaves and pine straw
Nature has a way of flashing its smile
at the perfect moment

Some suffering is only temporary
Some synchronicity is free of all charge
Some soldiers reunited with their family today
Some shoulders will prove to carry the weight


*Scott Thomas Outlar*

# Justifications

The repairman couldn't repair your sink.
*Not everything can be fixed.*
*Be grateful you've got a sink.*

The rain slips through your shoes and soaks your socks.
*Take time to enjoy the wonder of nature.*
*Are you sure those are your socks?*

Your favorite TV show has been taken off the air.
*Rest assured, "they" took it off for a good reason,*
*probably because no one understood the jokes.*

The neighbor ran over your dog.
It always savaged his garbage.
*How do you think it makes your neighbor feel?*

Your favorite song has a new skip in it.
*Honor the laws of decay and loss.*
*Of course, had you taken better care of your CD player and*
*CD --*

On the bus you get hard glares or giggles.
*Give a glare for a glare, a giggle for a giggle.*
*At least somebody noticed.*

Your friend didn't invite you to his big party.
*He was scared to say directly, "you're not my friend."*
*Besides, there wasn't enough toilet paper.*

Loud neighbors have moved in behind the thin walls.
*Your quiet attracts and disturbs them.*

There's nothing on the menu you care to eat.
*Picky, picky, picky.*
*So, pick a number, any number.*

Your girlfriend found her soul mate on her holiday.
*She liked what she got and she really got a lot.*
*She's better off without you.*

The boss would like to fire you.
*You're supposed to be a profit center, not overhead.*
*When was the last time you added value?*

Has anyone told you that your breath is simply atrocious?
*That's what happens when you swallow your anger.*

A strange creature won't budge from your chair
*The sign said "no standing" and there was nowhere else to*
*sit.*

A stain simply won't come off your best shirt.
*Freeze the shirt, then chip off the stain with a chisel.*

Your mother called.  She said she never loved you.
*You reap the bitter weeds you sow.*

Doctors can't find what's wrong with you.
*Take a multiple vitamin supplement.  Try another doctor.*

No one cares if you live or die.
*If your song is lame, you have only yourself to blame.*


*Paul Brucker*

# Human

Accepting the need to feel loved
does not make you weak
does not make you foolish
it makes you human.


*Roz Weaver*

# Escalation

If ever a time comes to whisper peace be with you,
it should be now. Words breezing gently into another's ear.
Eyes full of hope and joy for the promise of a changed
world.

If ever a time happens to speak aloud that you are my
friend, it should be now. Hands extended in amity,
words said with utmost sincerity, atonements completed
and conscience wiped clean.

If ever a time requires making music, it should be now.
Feeling the rhythm, the dance of the universe, all sounds
for all seasons, sing, strum, beat, slide, blow, and chant.

If ever a time should be for walking, it should be now.
Wandering in a beautiful world, learning as you go,
strolling past the familiar and unfamiliar.

If ever it comes to pass that we should run, it should be
now. Feeling the mirth and gaiety of the wind in our hair.
Hastening without fear of doom, toward an ecstasy both
spiritual and absolute.

If ever we desire to jump and shout for the joy of living,
it should be now. Loudly celebrating with body, mind,
heart, soul. Let it start here with us.


*Linda Imbler*

# Why

I will not die.
I will not die.
I will not die
until
I have unloaded
a hundred poems
to tell me why.

I will not die.
I will not die
until
I have unloaded
a thousand songs
on why
I will not die.

*Lynn White*

# Alternate Universe

In fever I fell
Into a horizontal parallel
A lateral coextending plane
Where Heaven is defined
As almost Hell

Where love,
Is how one learns to hate
And God is always to blame
Where reality is an abstract fancy
And hope is none

Purgatory the hereafter
It is here, and it is done


*Kimmy Alan*

# Who You Are

Is who I am
You are me
And I am you
We are humans
With black skin
Or white skin
We are still human
Like sky full of stars
Like the sea full of fish
We are together humans
Though different
Still you and I
Are human
Both you and I
Come from Adam and Eve
We are human
The same human
You and I
One race.


*Monsif Beroual*

# Perception Manifest

The beauty in your daily life
is the perception within your soul!

A truth contained inside your heart
is the brightest of them all.

Allow it all to flow forth
like a mighty river to the sea.

Gaze upon what's far above
the stars will set you free.

Standing on a principal mountain
a majestic deer begins to graze.

Your vision of the moment
occurring just beyond the haze.

A drop of moisture upon your cheek
from clouds within the sky

Booming sounds of distant thunder
sovereign eagles gliding by

Sweeping realization manifest
presented in broad view

Whatever you've been searching for
has always been with you.


*Matthew John Lambert*

# Building Gods

We are spilt onto this canvas for reasons
of which we do not know. That is,
if there even is a reason in the first place.
Our ancestors created creation by conjuring
Gods and inventing an interpretation of Existence
based on their limited knowledge of
Nature coupled with Imagination.
These false focal points have led Humanity away
from the True Universal Realities which Existed
long before Mankind achieved its current state of Sentience
and ignored the already-Existing Existence into which they
were born, thus, causing a flawed understanding of the
Natural world which manifest and carved itself into the
bones and wombs of the false manmade  societal
Consciousness of the oncoming Millennia.


*Heath Brougher*

# Be Peace

Our interpretation of reality blinds us,
miracles are just waiting to be born.
Reflections from others surround us,
intelligence is within us, not formed.
Circumstances try to entrap our minds,
detachment from chaos, sets us free.
Storms appear, to light our souls on fire,
a higher purpose shall bring us peace.

*Debra McLain*

# Essential Existentialism

The perfect dichotomy
is the human experience
Stitched in perfection,
my biological vehicle
housing my essence,
my essential self.
my eternal self.
Suffering these slings
of physical form,
sparring within it
to retain purity of
soul, in my unholy
times and places
Sparring with ego,
to hear the prodding
of my thirsty heart,
my body falling away
year after finite year
Infinite soul looming
larger in the distance
while existing within
this,
the perfect dichotomy.


*Brenda-Lee Ranta*

*Heartfelt thanks*
*to all the contributors*
*for sharing their deepest thoughts on*
*the meaning of life.*

# Creative Talents Unleashed

Creative Talents Unleashed is an independent publishing group that offers writers an opportunity to share their writing talents with the world. We are committed to fostering and honoring the work of writers of all cultures. Our publishing group offers writing tips to assist writers in continued growth and learning, daily writing prompts and challenges to keep the writers mind sharp, marketing and events, as well as a variety of yearly publishing opportunities. We are honored to be assisting writers in the journey of becoming published authors.

## Creative Talents Unleashed

www.ctupublishinggroup.com

### For More Information Contact:

Creativetalentsunleashed@aol.com

*Website: www.ctupublishinggroup.com*

*Blog: www.creativetalentunleashed.com*

28699214R00066